SCHOOL'S IN

SCHOOL'S IN

LARRY BARNETT

Library of Congress Control Number: 2009904903
ISBN: Hardcover   978-1-4415-3844-4
                   Softcover   978-1-4415-3843-7

This book was printed in the United States of America.

To order additional copies of this book, contact:
Xlibris Corporation
1-888-795-4274
www.Xlibris.com
Orders@Xlibris.com
62544

Contents

JESUS HANGED ON THE CROSS SO THAT WE WOULDN'T BE LOST. REMEMBER THAT THEY DID NOT TAKE HIS LIFE, HE GAVE IT FOR US. SO NEVER THINK THAT EVERYTHING THAT YOU HAVE IS BECAUSE OF YOUR GREATNESS. NO IT IS NOT BECAUSE OF OUR SIMPLE SKILLS. WE HAVE WHAT WE HAVE BECAUSE GOD GAVE IT TO US. AND JUST LIKE HE GAVE IT HE CAN TAKE IT JUST THE SAME.

ALWAYS REMEMBER THAT POTNA.

BIOGRAPHY

Thank You, Jesus

MR. LARRY BARNETT Jr. was born on February 16, 1980, in Saginaw, Michigan. He is the only child of Mr. Larry Barnett Sr. and Ms. Dianne Johnson-Barnett. A car hit Larry Junior on April 25, 1986, two months after his sixth birthday. The accident left Larry paralyzed from his neck down. The proper term for this injury is a level C1-C2 spinal cord injury. The car accident left Mr. Barnett with a broken spine at the base of his skull, but it did not break his will.

Larry Barnett Jr. went through five months of rehab in Denver Children's Hospital in Denver, Colorado. When he returned home, he went through a full year of more rehab before returning to school.

Larry's parents had to fight before he was allowed to attend public school and attend regular educational classes. His parents won that legal battle, which gave him the right to attend public school.

Larry Barnett Jr. was blessed to attend regular classes at Brunkow Elementary, Ricker Middle School, and he graduated from Buena Vista High School at age of nineteen in 1999. Larry Junior was given the chance to speak at his high school graduation, and being the person that he is, he jumped at the opportunity.

Mr. Barnett is a former eight-time member of the National Honor Society. He was put in the Who's Who Book of American Graduates. He received the True Knights Award when he finished school. He also received the Courage Award at the end of his eleventh-grade year.

Larry Junior is currently a student of Delta College. His major is business administration. Mr. Barnett has been running his own corporation for the past two and a half years. This business is called 3DO Stylez LLC. The purpose of this corporation is meant to positively affect the minds of people and to show them that people like Mr. Barnett do have a contribution to the entire world.

Larry Junior is a former member of the Think First Program. This organization gave him the chance to speak at Saginaw High School and Bridgeport Middle School. Mr. Barnett also spoke at the Delta College Awards Program. Although he has not spoken publicly since 2005, he has not lost his drive or his passion.

Mr. Barnett is also the founder of the Will on Wheels Technical Ability Center and the End Tyme Soldier. The purpose of these nonprofit organizations is to give all people of all ages, races, and backgrounds a mental and emotional outlet. Although there are many projects under the 3 DO Stylez LLC umbrella this is Mr. Barnett's passion. Without God this wouldn't be possible.

Thank You.

Inspiration

Today's tomorrow's ain't promised
so face them now
'Cause our forever has a limit
seek to replace the hows
The thought of overcoming challenges
is fuel to fire
Because if designated fate
fear is useless now
Disbelieving is unachieving
worthless thoughts
The key to being a winner
learn to work with loss
Determination and drive
are enough to pass
But keep focus on your goal
is enough to last.

Qur'an Abdul-Shaheed Ali
(October 5)

REALITY CHECK

THIS WORLD IS not set up for my people to succeed. When I say my people, I am not only talking about African Americans. I also mean people who are paralyzed in any way, shape, or form. Society thinks that blacks are only good for sports, music, and negative roles in movies. At the same time, they think cripple folks are good for nothing. Let's take a look at this for a second. In sports, how many black coaches do you see in any sport; how many black quarterbacks are in the NLF? Third thing, why did it take so long for a black man to win the Super Bowl, and when will it happen again? Don't get me wrong; no one loves sports more than me, especially the NFL.

I am just making the comparison between the two to make you see, for as many black coaches that we see, which is hardly any, there are less cripple people that are allowed to do anything. I'm a living proof of this fact. I am not the only one; there are a billion stories like mine and even worse than mine. The reason for my books is not just for success, although that is one very big motivator. I would be a liar if I said that it wasn't more than that; I want to give people like myself a voice. People, like my own dad, think that people who are paralyzed can't do anything unless someone else is in complete control – ain't that some crap? Please understand it is not easy for people like me to find other people who are willing to work hard for what they want.

Most young people have a zero ambition; they want all that life has to offer, but they don't want to work for it. They think that it will just fall out of the sky. Even when you pray, the next day, you gotta try. You can't wait for nobody to come down from the sky. You got to realize that the world's a test; you can only do your best and let them do the rest. Translation – God gave us the ability, so get to work and don't sweat the small stuff.

If someone asked me to name the top five songs that motivate me in order, they would go like this.

1. Nas – "Hate Me Now"
2. Nas – "Mastermind"
3. Kanye West – "Through the Wire"
4. T.I. – "Motivation"
5. Young Jeezy – "Put On"

Now I ask you, what is your motivation? Nothing that I say is meant to spark any controversy; all I want to do is get people to wake up and smell the coffee. Life is too short and unpredictable to waste on petty garbage.

Now let's go to school; let's get our PhD in life.

I will lift up mine eyes unto the hills, from whence cometh my help.

My help cometh cometh from the Lord, which made heaven and earth.

He will not suffer thy foot to be moved: he that keepeth thee will not slumber.

Behold, he that keepeth Israel shall neither slumber nor sleep.

The Lord is they keeper; the Lord is thy shade upon thy right hand.

The sun shall not smite thee by day, nor the moon by night.

The Lord shall preserve thee from all evil: he shall preserve thy soul.

The Lord shall preserve they going out and they coming in from this time forth, and even for evermore.

– Psalm 121

And there was born unto him seven sons and three daughters.

– Job: 1:2

I, Larry Barnett Jr., promise to be friends with Jared Cameron until the day I die.

I, Jared Cameron, promise to be friends with Larry Barnett until the day I die.

We promise!

3 DO STYLEZ LLC

Mission Statement – 2007

THE 3 DO Stylez LLC is committed to providing different forms of education and entertainment outlets to help open the minds of all residents in the city of Saginaw. This corporation provides several programs such as "The Will on Wheels Technical Ability Center" and the "End Tyme Soldiers" to help positively affect people of all races, background, and gender. This corporation is a nonprofit organization. The Will on Wheels is set up to educate all people about how to handle individuals with any type of disability through lectures and classes, as well as access to a computer center. The purpose of the End Tyme Soldiers is to positively reach the minds of the youth in Saginaw and give them an alternative to draw them away from violence.

Schools In

Life is filled with many hooks and turn and bends. That seems to have no end and even a full supply of so-called friends.

That will do you in.

When given the chance, but school is in my friend.

School is definitely in, so don't waste your time in the hallways of uselessness, get in the game, and proclaim your fame.

FOCUS

IN ORDER TO understand my train of thought, you need to put yourself in my position. You can't expect me to think like you because my life is not like yours. Never make the mistake of thinking that you can predict my next move because it's like I said before, just when you think you have the answer, I change the question.

Life is full of different kinds of people. This is what makes this world so beautiful. If you think that everyone should be like you, you are really screwed up, and please always remember that you cannot move ahead in life looking back. We need to say that the past just doesn't matter anymore.

This is what I am. This is what makes me. This is what I feel. This is my legacy.

I have only one direction and one speed, and that is full steam ahead, straight ahead. You cannot move forward looking back. Simply put, the past don't matter. Where you come from don't matter, and forget what people say.

Your path is up to God, and he has your life in his hands and that is all that matters.

SEPTEMBER 2, 2008

T HE WHOLE SCHOOL experience means a lot of different things to a lot of different people. To some people, school was the greatest experience in their lives, and they will give anything to go back and do it again. For others, school was just away to past time between weekends. Then you have the students that come to school and kiss every teacher's ass – you know the type. These people don't have to work very hard to get anything but kissing other's asses, and everything get handed to them whether they deserve it or not. I guess it is true what they say: It ain't what you know, it's whom you know anybody, and that's why I ain't got shit.

That leaves me to the next type of person. The type of person that works hard but still gets looked over for every opportunity. This is where the category I belong in, and the reason why I know I fit in this category because of twenty-two years of experience. Just about every situation I've been, no matter what it is, the odds are always stacked against me. And it has been this way ever since I survived the accident. The most doubters that I have ever faced actually begin from kindergarten so when I think about it, I have been fighting this fight since I was about five years old. So maybe that's why I was so comfortable in it sometimes, and sometimes it is the reason why I get tired of the fight. But if I don't fight, I don't survive, simple as that. Back on school, I will be the first to admit that my whole entire school experience sucked. The only good time I had was the day that I graduated and I didn't have to see those fake people anymore. If you are from BV High and you graduated in '99 and you are offended by the previous statement, that means you feel something and you're not robotic like you were, back in school. The people that were in my class, some were very nice (but not very many) while the rest of them were caught up in some kind of *Fantasy Island* fairy tale of what they thought their life was going to be.

But something that I always hear my mother and my godmother say is "Be careful whom you step on your way to the top because you might have to meet them same folks on your way down." This statement fits anyone from BV that graduated between the years of 1998 through 2002. As far as the rest of them go, I can't speak on that because I don't know them; but for the ones I do know, the ones that I came face to face, with regards to the above statement, if the shoe fits, wear it. But if it doesn't apply to you, don't be offended, don't worry about it.

If the people reading this think that I sound a little bitter, yeah, I am just a little bit, but not in the way you may think. I don't hate people, and I don't feel like people owe me anything. I don't wish my situation on anyone. I don't regret my life; in fact, I love life. But if someone came and asked me if there was any part of my life that I would like to change, I will tell them that the only thing I will like to change was the fact that I can't walk because other than that, my life has been incredible.

Please don't misunderstand what is being said when it comes to elementary school, middle school, and high school or college. I am not knocking any forms of education because you need education to make anything out of your life and to go as far as you want to go. Though I do not disrespect any learning institution, I do however believe that for all the things you learn in school, the real education does not begin until you step into the real world because in the real world, you are not protected by principles, teachers, or security guards – anything that you face in the real world, nine times out of ten, you have to deal with on your own. In most cases, the people that try to do you in are your so-called friends, whether it be business, money, depression, or relationships. In the real world, your problems are your problems, and other people really don't give a rat's ass about what you do.

Some people call this the school of hard knocks, but I choose to call it the school of the real. Because in this school, there is no graduation day; there is no party to celebrate your accomplishments. The only real celebration that you get is knowing that you have survived another situation and you are still alive to talk about it. In other words, through the fire, we are still alive. Too often people set their plans in motion with regard to how they want their lives to go. But I know from experiences that life doesn't work that way. Just look at me; do you really think that I planned to be paralyzed from the neck down? Of course not.

My plan was to be a regular kid, go to college one day, and make a lot of money in whatever field I choose, but I was thrown into this situation, and now I'm going to make the best out of it – simple as that. Trust me, if I can blink my eyes and be able to walk tomorrow, I would do it in a second, but you and I know both things are never that easy. If they were that easy, I would have never stayed in the hospital after my accident; hell, I would had never got hit, but I did and so I'm here. And now I have to deal with it because this the hand that I was dealt. But instead of playing the hand that I was dealt, I am going to pray to God and ask him to change my cards.

This is what I'm talking about when I say school for me didn't begin till after I graduated from Buena Vista High School. I can honestly say that all the stuff that I learned from the first grade till the twelfth grade does not apply to anything in my life today. From Brunkow Elementary all the way through BV High, not one time did they tell me how to cope with not being able to walk or how to deal with depression. Nobody told me that there would come a time in my life that I will feel like I wanted to die, and no one in those schools told me that when I got to my lowest point, there would be no friends around to help me dig out of that hole because like I said before, as wonderful as school is for everyone, it doesn't tell you how to deal with the real life.

The object of a school is to get young people prepared for college and then get them ready to go out into the real world so they can get a good job. But answer this question: Why are there so many degree holders that are jobless or homeless? Who says that just because you got a degree, you have the right to act an ass toward people. Just because you have a little piece of paper that means a whole lot, it does not make a person superior, but the chances are if you are an ass with a degree, you will still be an ass without one.

If it sound that I'm a bit frustrated, you are wrong because I am frustrated a lot for the simple reason that you have people in this world that are in college and are in the workforce, but they don't deserve it. I'm not saying everyone, but there is a very good percentage of folks that fit in this category. Then you have people like me that want to go to college who would love to work, but they take one look at me at my outer appearance and won't even give me a chance. Because of the distorted picture society has painted for them, not only does this apply for school and work, but it applies to friendships and relationships also. Tell me how can a world that is ready, willing, and able to except gay and lesbian relationship cannot be able to accept a man or a women who has a physical disability. Think about that, and tell me that's not backward. Cripple people are people to and deserve much respect as everyone else.

I don't think that people hate the disabled; I just think they overlook us. I believe, in their minds, they feel like we are none factors on regards to everything in a world – this is some bullshit. So many times during my school days, I felt like I didn't belong because I wasn't like the other kids. I didn't look like the others, I didn't sound like the others, and I did not think like everybody else. Because my situation was not or is not like everybody else.

Because of circumstances beyond my control, I had to grow up faster than everybody else. Someone once told me that it is not your age that determines if you are a man or not, but it is the situation that you have dealt within your life and how you come out of those situation determines if you are man or boy.

These are the lessons that stick with me; these are the things that have shaped and molded me into who I am now. You can go to school all of your life – these are called career students – and you can graduate from every level education that there is. But remember this, some people graduate, but still stupid. What good is all the education in the world if you don't have common sense to go along with that or you don't know how to treat people and you feel like people are less than you because they don't have what you have. Trust me, the ones that you underestimate will be the ones that take ya butt to school and give you a real reality check. It might sound off to most people, but the reason I feel the way I do is because I was never treated like everyone else. I never had an opportunity to drive myself to school or anywhere else for that matter.

I never had a chance to go on a job interview; I never had a chance to live on my own anywhere. I never ever had a girlfriend; its not that I don't want one because, believe me, I have tried harder than anybody else I know. It's just that most females see guys in a wheelchair as a nuisance, but that's not the point I'm trying to make. The point I'm trying to make is these are some of the things I have missed out on. Because of the way my life has played out to this point. It may sound simple to most, but believe me, it is not simple when you have never had this stuff. A lot of the simple things in life are taken for granted when you do them every day, but try to live a year or two without something that you have every day and see how you hold it together, or will you crumble in an hour or less.

People oftentimes tell me that I am better off without the things that I mentioned before I believe them but how do I rightfully know this if I never had these things. I put that on the same level as people never having kids but giving advice on how to raise kids. How would they know if they are not down in the trenches doing the work?

I respect your opinion, and I hear what you're saying, but I can't live my life based on someone else's interpretation. I didn't learn any of this stuff inside of a classroom. Sometimes you learn your best stuff after life kicks your butt. I am very grateful for every teacher that I had. They helped me to increase and gain knowledge about a lot of things. They challenged my brain in ways that I thought they could.

I have met a lot of cool people as well as a whole lot of jackasses along the way. In hindsight, the jackasses outnumbered the cool people by a huge margin. I have met people that were actually sad because I didn't fail. I have run into the people that doubted the most, but when the dust clears, they say, "I knew he could do it." I also met people that have been very supportive of my family and me since day 1. The reason why I chose to become a writer is because there are a lot I have to get off my chest as you can see.

The reason why I started my own business 3 DO Stylez LLC Will on Wheels Technical Support Ability Center is because I did the research about where I could work. And believe me, no one is hiring a man who is paralyzed from the neck down no matter how good his brain is. Would you?

When I was sixteen or seventeen years old, I read a book; the title of the book was *Looking Out for #1*. This book pretty much changed my whole outlook on life. It also changed the way I view people. This book showed me how to be successful; it also taught me that individuals around me, no matter if they're successful or not, will put themselves on a pedestal and will stop at nothing to make others around them feel small as possible or insignificant.

So at that point, after reading this book, I felt my best weapon was to chop them down before they chop me or anyone else I know down. After so many years of trying to prove how much better I was intellectually, I got kind of bored; and as I got older, after life kicked me around a lit bit, I realized that my philosophy sucked. As smart as I thought I was, it was always someone ready, willing, and able to top me in everything I tried to do. At that point I started to study people so that I could learn as many skills as I could fit into my brain. The reason why I'm telling you all this is because in order to understand a person who's physically disabled, you must know that everything that we do is 99 percent mental.

Since we can't use our bodies, we need to have some kind of control of our situation. Some people call this being manipulative, but they need to understand that when you're a full-grown man or woman that's in my situation you want to have some say over your own life. I guess that's why I've been kicked out of every advocate program that I've ever attended because those programs put up a front like they're for the physically disabled and they mean well, but those programs are set up by people who have full use of their bodies. At the risk of sounding like an asshole.

What can someone with full use of their body tell someone about how to enjoy life, which has been paralyzed for the last twenty years of their life? That's just like somebody who's been dating for two years telling a couple who've been married thirty years how to act in a relationship. It just doesn't work that way.

Sometimes people confuse my pain with bitterness. Let me inform you that there's a big difference between being hurt and being bitter. Let me assure you that I am the former, not the latter. A bitter person will sit all day every day and soak in his own sorrows, thinking of all the people they'd like to see hurt, just like them. A bitter person will also think of every little thing they have going on in their life. People call this a "pity party."

The reason I know all this is because that person used to be me. Emphasis on "used" to. I'm hurt, now when I think of my past, the only question in my mind is "Why was I singled out?" What I mean by this is I have a brain that works with no problem, and I thank God for that, but it have trapped in a body that's 99 percent useless. I've said it before, and I'll say it again. I want to walk again so bad that it hurts when I think about it. Circumstances beyond my or anyone else's control left me unable to live life the way I want to and know I could if I could walk. So here's the question I'm faced with – given my current situation, will I give up or will I press on? The answer is simple; I will use every disappointment and every failure to feed the fire inside. I will ride the hell this thing! "The home of the free, land of the brave," America, the beautiful, the land of opportunity – all that is great and wonderful as long as society thinks you are necessary. But what do you do? When things in the economy are so bad, they slowly begin to phase out just about every program set up to help people like myself. I'm not taking a selfish approach; I'm looking at the bigger picture.

There are over 6 million people in the Midwest along living with some kind of physical disability. What do people like us do when our state and government try to deny us the right to an education or to be part of the workforce just because they're afraid to think outside the box?

I completely understand that in order to have a regular job, you have to meet certain physical requirements. Folks like myself don't fit into the status quo, but please don't deny us the right to live like everyone else. Please don't shove us in a back room and just figure that we'll go away. Trust me, its not that easy. We'll keep getting louder and louder until someone hears our voice. I've been through it before, and I already know the play. I know what it takes to win. I know it'll take a lot of hard work, but I'll do anything I can to make sure people like me are allowed on a level playing field.

A while back, I took a couple of African American's history classes. One was the Black Experience taught by Professor Willie Thompson, the other was AA Literature taught by Professor Bill Ketcham. I took a lot from these classes, and I found the real sources of my angel. These two brilliant professors taught me: being a black man in America – it's designed for us to lose. We have work triple times as hard (plus some more) in order to even get our foot in the door. Once our foot is in the door, we have to work even harder to succeed. Even then, we still have to strive to hold on to what we have. These two men taught me a lot, but at the end of those classes, I had a question for them. I asked, "Since we know all this is working against us as black men, what will you do when you're a young black and paralyzed from the neck down?" All the intelligence you've shown people still is enough because you know deep down, they're looking at you, thinking, "Yeah, you're smart, but you're crippled." What do you do then – you have the answer? Because after twenty-two years and counting, I still don't know what's going on sometimes. I told you before everyone has a special date, place, and time that changed your life forever. Whether it be good or bad, that day will change your life. I told you in my last book, one of those dates for me was April 25, 1986. But it didn't end there; here's two more: May 10 and June 8, 2008.

In order for you, the reader, to fully understand the significance of these two dates, I must take you back to the beginning of when the string of the strange events started. Saturday May 3, 2008, between the hours of 8:00-9:00 p.m., I was at home hanging out with my best friend Jared while my mom and the rest of my family were at a church fashion show when the call came through around 8:45 p.m. It was my cousin Teyanna telling me that her seventeen-year-old nephew, my cousin Jerome, was just shot and killed. From that point, it was left up to me to track down the rest of the family and give them the bad news. You can probably imagine how difficult this must have been after all the thing my family had just been through. Just think about it: it's not exactly easy to tell someone over the phone that a loved one has just passed, especially when that loved one is seventeen years old. His death reminded everyone of his dad's murder back in 1996 when I was sixteen years old. I guess, for a moment, time felt like it stood still and it felt like 1996 all over again. Not just for me, but the whole entire family. What I mean is my cousin Betty lost her youngest son, then his son, which was her oldest grandson, and in almost the same way. But fast-forwarding to the rest of the week, it was basically just a regular week.

Routine remained the same, besides that fact that we were preparing to bury my little cousin. I was pretty much able to maintain some since of normalcy in my life until May 10, 2008. On this date, everything went haywire. Here's what happen: My mom, Aunt Gloria, cousin Sharnae, and myself were getting ready to load up to go to my cousin's funeral. The normal routine was Sharnae, me on my wheelchair, would lift and put me in the van, while Mom and Aunt Gloria finish getting dressed. Remember I said normal, but this time was different. I got on the lift and as I made it to the top, the lift began to stop. So I decided to tell Sharnae that, since the lift was acting up, she should let me back down so we could figure out the problem. But on the way back down, the lift froze about three and a half feet in the air. My chair began to roll. I fell face-first out of my chair onto the garage floor. I went one way, and my chair went the other before Sharnae or I realized it. So there I was facedown on the ground, trying to figure out what happened and how did it happen because after twenty-two years, I hadn't done this well over a million times, and I've never fallen from anything. Strange part about it, when I fell, I was never disconnected from my ventilator.

I do remember saying to God, "After all I've been through, I know I'm not going out like this, on the garage floor."

Just as I said, Mom came out from the house and was able to keep me breathing until the paramedics came. Once I got to the hospital, my biggest fear was the length of time I'd be there. Once everything checked out, I had nothing more than a few bumps and bruisers. Nothing more, or so I thought. They allowed me to come home. For about two to three weeks after that, I had a hard time getting my head back together. I couldn't stop thinking, what if things would've turned out different and I had stopped breathing? Or mom didn't make it in time? That would've been a wrap for LB Junior, but I'm still here. I can't go yet; I got a lot more people to torment. Besides that, I guess you can say I'm a writer now. I have a whole lot of opinions about everything, and the world is about to hear them all.

After weeks of struggling, I finally was able to relax. And I was getting ready to enjoy the spring and summer. The weather was getting hot, and I felt great until, uh oh! my back started hurting real bad and I began having more muscle spasms than usual. Some were so bad I felt like I was going to jump out of my chair. But no matter how bad it hurt, I try my hardest not to tell anyone just so I wouldn't have to go to the hospital. But I couldn't hide the pain for long. My mom eventually noticed also that I wasn't being myself. So finally on Thursday, June 5, she made me go to the hospital. They put me through a whole plethora of test. I'm talking about X-rays, CAT scans, ultrasounds, MRIs, blood cultures, and any other blood works that would show signs of an infection. The whole time they were testing, I was praying that I could come home instead of staying in the hospital.

So eventually after six hours at the hospital, they sent me home, but it was one catch. They didn't have all the results from the entire test. So the next day (which was Friday, June 6), I was doing a lot better, or so I thought. I was going through my daily routine of getting ready to get in my wheelchair when the phone rang about eleven thirty, and it was the hospital with the results from the test. The test read that because of an obstruction that was being caused by a kidney stone that wouldn't pass, I had a bladder infection that got into my bloodstream.

You must understand that infections like this are common with people with any type of physical limitations, especially quadriplegics. Any small blockage in our bodies will cause muscle spasms, and since we're not able to feel pain in that particular part of the body, the brain and nerves automatically send the pain's signal to the next best area. In my case, it was my shoulders and back. So they check me into the hospital late that night and told me that I'd be there three to four days tops. But those three to four days turned into twelve long days.

But that was the crazy part of my stay because what happened to me on day 2, I still couldn't wrap my mind around it. Sunday, June 8, the hospital brought in a kidney specialist. He decided because of the obstruction from the kidney stone, the best thing would be to put stint in to help clean out the infection. But in order to do this, they thought they had to put me to sleep. The reason why I say *thought* is because if you know anything about quads, you know we can't feel anything. So heavy sedation is always the very last resort. So they prepared me for the surgery, and before I knew it, they had me surrounded by a team of so-called experts who knew nothing of taking care of a person like myself. On the way into the OR, these overly smart people connected me to an oddly made ventilator. At that time, I became disconnected. If it weren't for this one nurse being able to read my lips, I would have died then. Till this day, I don't know her name, and I never saw her again after that.

But the way things took place, I will always see her as my angel that day. So the next thing I know, the surgery's over, and I'm waking up in my room with my family all around me. So I'm finally awake, talking to my best friend. And as we were talking, I began to have this funny feeling. My eyes got very blurry, and I got dizzy. Next thing I know, I wake up with people rolling my bed down the hall. I kept hearing weird alarms, and the words, code blue. I had no idea it was for me, so when I do wake up, my mom explained to me that I'd passed out. For a minute, they thought I wasn't going to make it. See, what happened to cause this chain of events to take place was too much anesthesia. You see, anybody with any sense already knows that you don't give a quad that much medicine, especially not one with low blood pressure. So after this very frustrating time, after my twelve-day stay in the hospital was finally over and I finally got back home, I had to readjust to being at home because in my mind I was still trying to figure out what happen and why was I there so long for a bladder infection.

But as time moved on, I figured it was all for the best, and I'm still here. That's all that really matters. These are the kind of things that happen in life that no amount of schooling can prepare you for. Last time I checked, there was no course called Life Experience 101. Even if they did have one, I'm 100 percent sure all the info would be wrong because you can't base life experience on the opinion of ten to fifteen people who've been spoon-fed their entire life. Again that would be like people with no kids, telling people with kids how to raise kids. Those types of things never work until you get down in the trenches and get your hands dirty.

What do you do when all of your hard work doesn't seem to be enough? What do you do when your best is just not good enough? Or what do you do when all of your blood, sweat, and tears don't seem to matter? You press on and you try to find ways to make the most of every situation good or bad. A lot of this has to do with motivation. I know where I want to be in life, and I keep that goal right in front of me for those times that I want to give up.

I look for inspiration in just about everything. It could be sports, movies, or my biggest motivation, music. A lot of people think that music is just senseless noise, and for the most part there, they are right. But every now and then, you might find an artist or two that has something to say in their music. Not every artist does this to me. There are a few that inspire me all day long. Artist like Nas, Kanye West, Akon, and Mos Def, just to name some. Some people think I'm weird because of my music selection. But in order to fully understand what those artists are saying, you must listen to their words.

I guess when I think about it, that's another life's lesson. In order to understand people that you meet, you must be willing to talk to them and listen to what they have to say because it may, or may not, have an excellent impact on your life. Either way, it goes that there is always something to be learned from other people because no matter what you think, you know there is always someone, somewhere, that knows more.

I know that to some people, it may look like I'm disrespecting school and the whole educational system but that is not it at all. My part is that once school is over, there is a whole lot of learning to be done. In most cases, once you graduate from high school or college, the learning process has just began. What do you do when you have a masters degree or a PhD but has no job? These are the kinds of question that a teacher or a professor cannot answer. We are always taught from the time that we are old enough to understand that school is the way, and it is. But what about for the people who are not acceptable in these institutes, what do we do?

The Michigan Rehabilitation Service told me that they would no longer pay for me to go to school because even if I got a degree, I will be no good in the workforce because of my physical situation. Let me back up for a moment and explain exactly what the Michigan Rehabilitation Service is supposed to do. The MRS was set up to help the physically disabled live normal lives, such as education, living arrangements, and jobs, in whatever fields that we chose. But somewhere along the line, this organization lost money instead of owning up to it and telling us what really happened. They decided to tell it like it is the fault of the disabled that we can't go to school or work. "Huge lie." People like myself do have a purpose, and we do belong in the society. But this problem doesn't end in Michigan; it goes right to the national government. When you hear presidential candidates give their speeches about their plans for the future, they never mention their plan for the physically challenged, like we don't exist at all. It's like we don't count no matter what we do or say, but I'm willing to bet anything that our votes counts on election dates, but our voices don't count.

I learned a long time ago that if you want something done right, you have to do it yourself. My dad isn't the best example for morals and righteousness. It's the one thing he does that I agree. With anything he ever does, he does it on his own. Because his theory is people let you down more oftentimes than not. You know what, I agree with him, 100 percent. He is somewhat of a loner, I guess, and that has always been me. I was never the most popular person in school, I never had the most friends, and I never came up with the month-to-month fads and trends that went on in school. If anything, I always went out my way to be different. I guess you can say, "Everything I'm not makes me everything I am." This simply means that, sometimes, it's what you don't do that makes you who you are. It's the reasons like this that made me come up with the Will on Wheels Center to give people like myself a voice to speak, as long as they want my commitment to this is undead. This is the quality I get from my mother, to never give up and to hold on to what you believe in.

No matter what insiders say, the things people need to understand about my mother is that she has always stuck with me through all the bull crop when everyone else belled out. So if and when I ever become successful, my mother will be treated like a *queen* before anyone else. No matter how off I sound sometimes, but she always have my back. But I guess I'm the kind of guy that only a mother can love. All right, you got me; sometimes, I act like an ass. But you tell me how many grown men out there are real enough to stand up and straighten their self on it. Some guys justify every stupid thing they do, blaming everyone else but them own selves. But remember, when you point one finger, its three pointing right back at you. Plain and simple, man, up and take responsibility for whatever you do good, or otherwise.

I told you earlier that everything I learn in school doesn't apply to what I'm doing now. But I did learn a few valuable lessons, but they didn't come in the classroom. What I learned in school was decision can make or break you. There are some things you get into in school that your parents can't help you out of. Like when you make the choice to get into with the teacher, and that particular teacher holds your grade in their hand, and no amount of talking will make them change their mind. You just get to be able to accept what coming to you or when you make the choice to skip class when you know it's a very important test being given – that dumb choice is all on you. Another thing school taught me was to never go into any situation without knowing the facts. Because if you do, you're asking for a butt kicking; in other words, choose your battles wisely. When you know you don't have a chance to don't give up, just save that battle for when you are more equipped to handle it. Because there is one thing I don't handle very well, and that's losing. Believe me, I have lost my share of battles, and I have won some too. Although I have more loses than wins, I never stop fighting. But I heard Michael Jordan say, "Before you learn how to win, you must learn how to lose first." And that is the process

I am going through now. And believe me, it is not very far, but I will be standing when the smoke clears. I believe that God has me on a path that I need to be on in order to succeed. My steps are ordered by the Lord. Sometimes that's hard to swallow, but that is the way it needs to be if I want this thing to be right. God could have taken me a long time ago if he wanted to, but it's clear to me now that after a car accident, broken spinal cord, in and out of a coma, falling off of a van lift, and getting code blue called on me in the hospital, and I'm still alive. If I can go through all that and still be breathing, it is safe to say I'm here for a reason.

Wow, I have a purpose. People don't understand just how long it took me to get to this revelation. All through high school, I'd sit and watch a few people I knew make preparations for after graduation, such as college choices, career choices, or just making moves toward their future. I would sit and wonder what does the future hold for someone paralyzed from the neck down. I didn't really believe that college was the place for me because even if I got my degree, which, in my personal opinion, it is nothing more than a glorified piece of paper that only gives you access into a society of folks who're out of touch with what reality really is. And if you disagree with me, please tell me why so many degree holders are jobless unless they're the underqualified son, daughter, or godchild of some other big-time executives?

But that's another story for another time. Either way it goes, if I had my degree, it wouldn't change societies opinion about the disabled. I know because I'm already dealing with trying to get back in college without having the State of Michigan agreeing to pay for it because of my physical situation. To tell you the truth, for those first five years after graduation, I always felt that I was spinning my wheels in the mud (so to speak and no pun intended), until God revealed it to me that the way to get my point across is I needed to let the world hear my voice. I guess that's why I decided to start writing; I consider it my personal therapy session.

This is my opportunity to make my impact on society. Will it help? I guess only time will tell, but I won't stop until I make some kind of move. My newest game plan will mirror that of the greatest man ever in science Steven Hawkins: "Never panic, but always proper." Because when he was diagnosed with the disease that eventually took his speaking ability, he developed a method to communicate through computers. So this means even if I never get to see the success of those books, they'll help someone else coming up behind me and make their path easier. Guess you can say that this is my legacy. Legacy isn't meant to be taken lightly. That's why I consider this to be the most important thing I've ever done. The definition of insanity is to do something the same way, over and over, expecting a different result. It's time to change the game plan and get a fresh playbook on life.

After a problem has been stated, the way to solve it isn't by continuing to go over the same thing over and over because after a while, it becomes redundant. After a problem has been discovered at that point, it's time to get together and come up with a solution. No one wants to hear what he or she does wrong over and over. We both know what the situation is; now let's talk about how to fix it. Just like with the country. Everyone knew at the beginning of the last administration where our country was headed, but they wait until everything is in hell before they try to dig it out. All I'm saying is when you see trouble on the horizon, don't wait until after it kicks your butt to do something. Get up and make preparations to deal with it head-on. You may not win every fight, but at least you didn't roll over and let the situation whoop you. Success comes with a serious price you have to be willing to fight with everything you have to make it to the top of the mountain. You also have to be willing to sacrifice just about everything to get where you want to be. The definition of success is a favorable outcome. This doesn't happen overnight. Anything built fast is sure to crumble fast.

After all, people always say, "Rome wasn't built in a day." Too many times in our society people become successful and forgot all about where they come from. The areas that made them who they are and what they are. I call these people "users" because they claim the place as if it was their real home. But when they get on their feet, they leave home and disrespect the very place they once loved so much, or did they? Let's not make any mistakes about it. I'm from Saginaw, Buena Vista Township, by way of Daniel Heights Housing Projects. These are the places that made me who I am right now, today.

I'm not going to paint the picture that everything is hunky-dory in Saginaw. Just think about it; this is the place where I got hit by a car and where I've had countless aches, pains, and broken hearts. But

I wouldn't change it for nothing in the world. Besides all that, when you think about it, what home city is perfect anyway? If anybody says there is, they're nothing more than a United States liar.

Don't get me wrong; I used to be one of those people that couldn't wait to get out of Saginaw. But as I got a little older and was able to travel a little bit, I realized all those other places that I once thought were so great only looked like that from the outside. But when you got up close, they have turmoil also. When you think about it, it may be worse. At least at home I'm in my comfort zone and I've got a support group. Saginaw, there's no place like home. How else you explain so many people they've dogged the place, running back here every chance they get. It took me a while to learn how to appreciate my hometown. The biggest wake-up call came when I started 3 DO (Third Dimension Oasis). The thing that made me open my eyes was all the support that I got at a few of my events. It was so great that words can't even explain what I was feeling. I remember sitting in the back of the first concert I held and watching the crowd's reaction. The thought came to me that maybe I was on the right track, and if I wanted to make a name for myself, what better place to start than good ole Saginaw, Michigan.

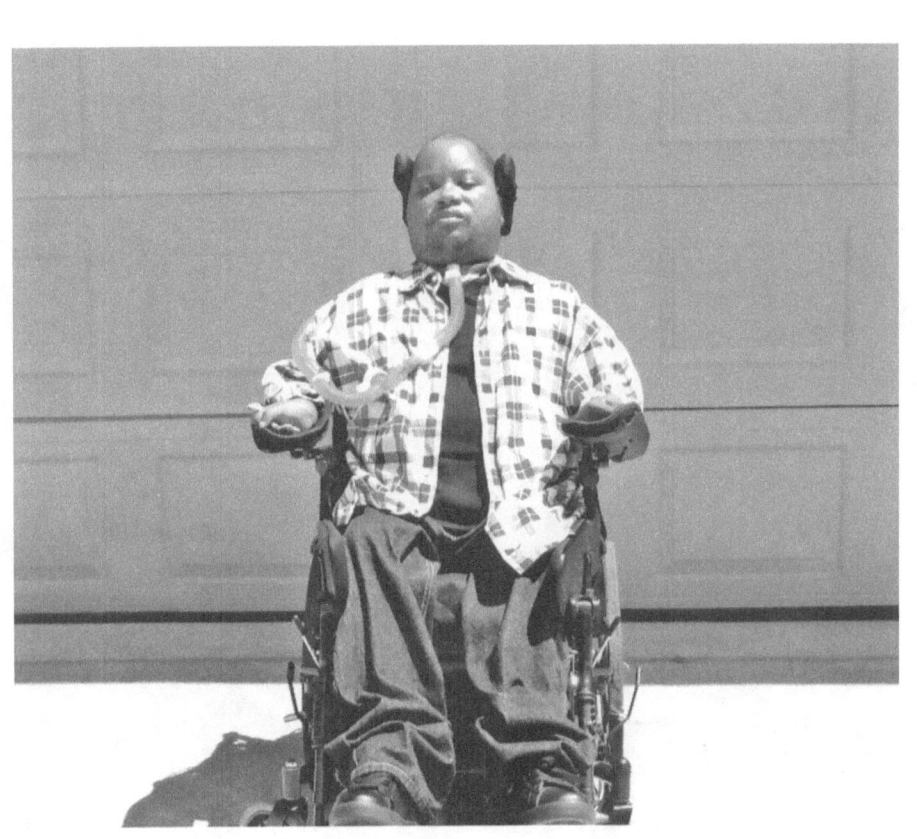

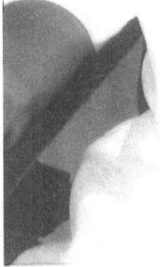

EDUCATION

◀ **INSPIRATIONAL GRADUATE:** Wheelchair-bound Larry Barnett, Jr. addresses his graduating class during commencement ceremonies at Buena Vista High School in Saginaw, MI. Though paralyzed from the neck down since he was struck by a car at age 6, the feisty 19-year-old endured surgery, intensive therapy and legal battles to enable him to attend regular school classes and graduate with his fellow classmates. He was awarded the high school's True Knight Award in tribute to his valor, courage and perseverance. Barnett plans to major in computer science. He will enter Delta College this fall and later plans to continue his studies at Michigan State University. He told his fellow graduates: "God allowed me to be placed in this situation. I can succeed through Him and anyone who has obstacles can do the same. There are no excuses, only people who make them."

People complain too much about Saginaw, but my first response to that is "If you don't like it, do something to change it, or just leave, bastards." I tell people that complain about my city. Sometimes it isn't the place, it's the person. Even if you move away, you still must take you with you. If you suck, you just suck. Don't blame a city for all of your life's problems. Don't get me wrong; sometimes a change of environment is a good thing. But in order to fully change your life's situation, it takes a little more focus, hard work, and dedication than just a change of location. If you have a special talent, skill, or ability, make it work for you. In order to get where you want to go. Everyone has a different view and opinion about the place he or she is from. I'm going to step aside for a moment and let you get a look at some of these other opinions on life, school, home, and different experiences what've impacted folks' lives. You never know you just might see some of yourself in this book.

Life is a class: school, being the world, is where the lessons take place. Some lessons are easier and almost second nature to some, and a living hellish nightmare to others. It all depends on the individual's intestinal fortitude. If it's in you, it's in you; if it ain't, it ain't. But you'll never know until you're present (like a child's acknowledgment of being in class). I didn't like or care for school coming up. Not because of my peers or it wasn't cool, I just didn't care for the shit. But just because I was fooling – and things of that nature – don't mean I didn't soak up every particle of what I needed to survive. I did and do now because, as I previously said, life's the class and the world is the school. The bells about to ring at any time; you gonna be ready for class?

My sister Keta says that high school was the greatest experience of her life. She says that it taught her different perspectives of life and the importance of making proper decisions that can make or break your entire future. She also says that high school was the place where she first learned that everyone's different, and as a society, we can't expect people to see things our way and respect each other's opinion. We must agree to disagree sometimes. My cousin Spanky told me that when he was in high school, he learned to break away from the shelter that's sometimes put up by our parents to help protect us, and whatever decision he made from that point on, good or bad, would make him stand up and be a real man and make him understand what responsibility really is. For my cousin Ericka, it was little different. She was a cheerleader and a homecoming and prom queen. She participated in everything. At the same time, she was a very hard worker, and that holds true still today.

As you can see, different people have different outlook and opinions on life and school. No one is 100 percent right or wrong. We're all just different. That's what makes the world go round. It would be a pretty boring place if everyone talked, looked, acted, or felt the same. In fact, the poem at the beginning of this was written by my mother; and in my personal opinion, it's the realist view you can have because at the end of the day, it really does come down to being able to recognize what real and what is fake. Life sometimes can present itself like a beautiful mirage. But as you get closer, it can turn into a real-life Wes Craven story. But sometimes, in real life, it can feel like pain and suffering will never end. But if it became, trouble don't last always. Believe it or not, when we're struggling, sometimes that could be a sign that we are headed in the right direction. I know it sounds crazy, but everything in life can't be dealt with logically. Sometimes, in order to make it through a situation, you have to throw out all logic and just go for what you know. Sometimes, you'll find yourself in a situation that make no sense whatsoever, but you must understand that it's only a test, and the trials that you face will only build character so that God can prepare us for the next level. Remember, God can't give us too much, too fast; we wouldn't be able to handle it. We might get the big head, and then we'll really be in trouble. I know what some of you are thinking, "I have a plan"; but from me to you, let me say that plans never work. Because if they did, do you honestly think that it was my plan to be crippled? Do you think I planned on losing my grandma and auntie to cancer in the last three years? Do you even think that I thought I would lose my cousin Robert to senseless violence? It's a good idea to have a plan and that's what we're taught in school, but it's like what the Boy Scouts say always, "Be prepared and always expect the unexpected." Now, that's life.

One of the most difficult parts of life is learning how to deal with reality and accepting a situation for what it really is. Because it's so easy to trick our minds into believing a lie; because to be honest with you, it's easier to live in a fantasyland than it is to deal with the truth. For example, when people are in a relationship, even though it might be the worst relationship ever, he or else will stay miserable just because they're afraid of being alone. Some people will stay just to save face because they're afraid of what friends and family might say. The hardest thing to do in the world sometimes is facing reality. Take me for example, no one made me go out into the street. I understood exactly what I was doing. And although no one is really to blame for the accident, here I am, almost twenty-three years later, and I deal with the consequences every day. Strange enough, the older I get, the more it hurts. I must reiterate that the pain I go through, I do not wish on my worst enemy. People should not have to go through the mental anguish that I go through every day. It's hard to deal with the fact that I'll never live a normal life. I'll never walk again. But no matter how hard it hurts, I can't allow my current situation to deter my dreams.

No matter what people say or do, forward progress is a must. If you're in my way, no matter who you are, you will get rolled over. It sounds harsh, but that's just the way it is. When you think about it, the hardest reality in the world to deal with is when family members turn their back on you and act like you don't exist. But the second you begin to taste even a little success, they want to come out the woodwork and act like they've had your back all the time. My attitude toward them is "Leave it like it was before the success, because I am still me, and you're still you." The love you're showing now isn't sincere, it's a front. I don't like fronts. Be one-way with me all the time. It's like what my godmother always says, "People don't feel about you the way you feel about them." And if people act funny toward you now, it's the way they felt all the time because people can only pretend for so long before the real them comes out. But for a person in my situation, loyalty is very important because we put a lot of stocks into what people tell us.

Because we depend on them to come through for us and they don't, the letdown is great. Not because we try to put unrealistic expectations on folks, it's really just because when you're disabled, it's not a whole lot to look forward to, and we have already been let down so much we look for a little shred of hope in just about everything. Not making any excuses, I just want to make everyone aware. I'm the type of man that happens to believe that I can make a difference right from my wheelchair. I don't discriminate. Everything I say, do, and write is meant for everyone. No matter if you're disabled, able to walk, black, white, or whatever; I want every one to get something out of what's being said even if you have a negative opinion. Let it be known so we can sit down and talk and possibly come up with a better solution that'll benefit everyone. I'm not afraid to break away from the norm and think outside the box. Just think about it, what part of my life says normal. Besides that, after a while, normal and average starts to get boring. I make a lot of sports references when I write or speak because, just like music, sports motivate me. If you pay any attention to sports, you know that you do whatever it takes to win. No, I am not talking about cheating, even though someone once said, "If you ain't cheating, you ain't trying." And it's only called cheating when you lose. But when you cheat and, win it's called scary. When I talk about doing whatever it takes to win, I mean go all out and never give in. Like I said before, you won't win every battle, but it'll be a battle well fought.

There are three things in life: that's rejection, quitting, and – I absolutely loathe – losing. But somehow, one way or another, these things always seem to make their way into day-to-day life. You never really have any say whether or not the first two will take place or not. It's almost inevitable you're going to lose sometimes because losing builds character. No matter what you try, you're going to get rejected from time to time. No matter if it's on the job, at school, at home, or in your personal life. But rejection happens even to the best of us. But the thing that bothers me the most more than losing and rejection put together is quitting. You all have heard the old saying "A quitter never wins and a winner never quits" – it sounds pretty good. But it means nothing if you don't apply it. I know that it's sometimes easier said than done. Believe me, I know. I'm the poster child for it.

I know what it's like to think that life is nothing. I've been to the deep dark lonely place called depression. When it feels like the only way out is suicide. And I've thought about giving up so many times that I've lost count. But thank God he pulled me out of that place just in the nick of time. He let me know that when we talk defeat, that's exactly what the devil wants. That's how he tries to destroy us, attack the mind with every negative outlook on everything in life. Once the mind is flooded with all this garbage, then he go in for the kill. But God is about life, not death. After all I've been through, I'm not going to give the devil any more satisfaction. It's not always your age that determines whether you are an adult or not, it's the way you deal with the situations you go through; that determines your maturity in life. Just imagine this for a second: waking up one day not being able to breathe on your own, not being able to walk, and not being able to live life the way you want to. Here's the question: What would you do? Would you crumble? Would you give up? Or would you ask God to give you the strength to deal with it and go through it and get on with living life?

I've been in the presence of both kinds of people, those who give up and those who roll on and keep living life. Believe me, as a person who have been on both sides of the fence, there's definitely something to be learned by both groups of people. I've been fighting this battle since '86, and each day is different. Some days I'm up, some days I'm so low that if feels like I'll never bounce back up. But somehow I always make it through. It may sound strange, but sometimes it is the smallest thing in the world that helps me out. It could be playing video games, watching sports, talking to family and friends, or music. But it's always something not to mention the people who're around me will never let me get too far down. They always seem to figure out a way to shove me out of it. Sometimes their methods could piss me off. But they don't care; they just don't want to see me going through any unnecessary self-imposed stress. There are a lot of things that this world has to offer that I'd love to experience, but because of my current situation, I'm very limited, but I'm able to educate myself on a lot of things because of travels through the mind.

Because I'm physically disabled, it gives me a hard time to think about just about everything. By doing this, I'm able to understand a lot more than the average twenty-eight-year-old. I told you before that I grew up around a lot of older people, and just by sitting and listening, I was able to absorb a lot of knowledge and understanding. Yeah, sometimes, I would be bored out my mind. It's the stuff I learned when I was a kid that helps me still today. I'm not going to bore you with all the major and minor details of what I do and don't know, but I'll tell you this: The tings that are going on in today's society are nothing new. Basically, what I'm saying is in today's world, everyone is struggling because of the economy. But where I come from, struggle is just a way of life.

Everyone wants to run around and blame everyone else for his or her problems; but, exactly, in order for real change to take place, you must work on yourself before you help anyone else. The way things are going in this world, sooner or later, we're going to need to depend on one another for help. This was a very tough lesson for someone like me to learn because when it comes to change, I'm the most stubborn person ever. I guess that's why God puts this lesson in our lives to break us of our habits and make us realize that his way is the only way.

The hardest lesson that I ever had to lean actually came in church. No, I'm not about to bash church, I just want to give you what my experience has been. Please realize that it's not my intention to tear down anyone; that's not me. I just want to share light on the subject from my perspective. I've been in church all my life since before I was born until now from St. Luke's Temple COGIC to my current church Lighthouse Memorial. Believe me I've learned a lot of valuable lessons from the Bible.

Whenever I'm going through some hard times, I always make it through because of God's word. I'll never take that for granted, but the one lesson that hurt me the most is when I learned that healing isn't for everyone. I've been in services where I've seen people healed, but at the end of the day, I was still unable to walk; and I began to question a lot of things, and some of the answers I received really shocked me. I began to say is that God's answer, or is it a man-made answer? Made to sound really good, but when you break it all down, there's no real substance to it. For example, I asked someone why hasn't God healed me because I know he can do it? The answer they gave me was because I didn't want it bad enough. What! I don't want it bad enough? People have no idea how bad I want to walk. If it was up to me, I would've walked out the hospital the same day I was hit. Besides that, doesn't the Bible say that all it takes is faith the size of a mustard seed? Since that's what it says, that's what I choose to believe. I don't mean to be disrespectful, but I rarely take anybody's word for it – just because they hold a certain title, because certain church folks will take God's word and twist it to make it fit their own agenda. If you're a member of a church, don't buy into that agenda. Some leaders will kick you out of that church and will call you rebellious for not drinking the "Kool-Aid," so to speak. If I'm not mistaken, God doesn't make us do anything. He reveals things to us and then it's up to us to follow him or face the consequences.

I'm choosing to follow him. Because what do, I got to lose, right? That one experience really broke me down for a while. But then I was reminded of something I heard years ago: "God wants to break me, shake me, like a sculpture, to use me for his *glory* in my culture. I'm in this till I'm out. So hit me for my trials, hear me for my faithfulness, hit me for the Lord Jesus Christ who I represent."

Roosevelt "Booba" Barnes is my direct connection to music. Music is very much a part of who I am. The man named Boob is my granddad. Even though I only met him once when I was three years old, I feel a strong connection with me because of music. You see, Granddad was a blues musician and recorded a couple CDs and toured Paris, France, and various other places before he passed away in 1996. His vocal and musical skills were passed down to my mother, Dianne Johnson-Barnett. The best gospel singer I ever heard. From the Mississippi Delta to Saginaw, Michigan, now you have me, Larry Barnett Jr. I can't sing or play any instrument, but I have a very deep passion for music. That's why I created 3 DO. Please don't get it twisted; 3DO is a record label / production company and anything else that I've done in the past was nothing more than a way to help get my business boosted. Because of the tract in my throat, I'm unable to do a lot of things vocally. That's why I choose to express myself through writing, which, in my personal opinion, is just another form of art, depending on who you are and who you ask. I write because it gives me a platform to show my artistic side. I came up with 3DO for the same reason, but instead of me being an artist, I can put others up front so that they can have an opportunity to display their own experience. What people don't realize is there's a lot of talent in my city. But it goes unrecognized because we're not Detroit, Chicago, or New York. I don't mean any disrespect, but I feel so good about the talent around here that I know we can hang with the best of 'em. We call it Sag Nasty round here. I'm going to rep it no matter how far up the latter, I make it even if I never make it at all. Somehow, someway, people will hear about what we have to offer.

There are a lot of talented people from around here that have tasted success. But they get famous and claim Detroit. I understand that years ago you had to be from a big city to make it, but what happens when you do make it and you still say nothing about where you're really from. If I'm not mistaken, that's a hypocrite. Besides that those GA cats don't do it, so why should we? For so many years, I felt really unnecessary; but since I started my business, I feel like I have some direction because now I can express what I'm feeling without any restraints. I can express out if I want to. As long as I continue to surround myself with the right folks, this biz will be okay.

But if I don't, I'll be my only obstacle. Life is one gigantic revolving door of education, and with each new turn comes new learning experience. We must take each turn and learn the most that we can. Always remember that each test comes to make us stronger. I mean, if you couldn't handle it, God won't give it to us. Never make the mistake of thinking that you've got it all figured out. The moment you do that, you'll be consumed by your own life's situations. Young people kill me with which they say that they're going to be the one that breaks the family curse. Whatever those curse maybe. They just might be the one to do so. But never get so arrogant with it that you think that everyone else in the family is dumb. Always remember that it's because of their sacrifices you're able to have the opportunities that you do have. So many times we hear young people say they can't wait to get grown.

What they don't realize is the older they get the harder it gets. Take it from me, being grown ain't crazy. People have no idea how many times I wish that I had a *Back to the Future* style time machines just so I can go back and do a whole lot of stuff over, but that's only fantasy. This is reality; in reality, there are no reset buttons. When you mess up, you just mess up. The only thing that you can do is to hope to make it right one day.

People get caught in their own *Fantasy Island* fairy tale ideology of what they think their life really is like. News flash! Your life's not liked that! The life you're pretending to live belongs to someone else. All you can hope to do in this lifetime is the best you can be. While you being yourself, don't step on anyone else, thinking that you're better; believe me you'll get chopped down to size real quick. In a way, I guess it's necessary for us to fall on our butt sometimes just to keep us honest.

I used to say that I'd give anything in the world to walk again and people always would say, "Be careful what you ask for, 'cause you just might get it." When it comes, you might have to give up something else to get what you want. It's going to sound crazy, but them people are absolutely right. I'm not willing to give up something that means a lot to me just to get something else because, after weighing the cost, maybe it wouldn't be worth it. Just to be able to walk again. Allow me to explain myself. I'm not saying that I like being crippled. What I'm saying is I'm learning to be content in my situation. I understand now that God has me here for a reason. It doesn't matter if I see it or not. Everything is working out for my best. I don't want to be one of those people who have an obtuse view on life, looking through the lenses of a pair of some drunken goggles. I want to see life for what it really is – a learning experience.

I have enough passion to succeed at anything. My heart beats with fury of lo lions on the prowl. All this means nothing without directions. My disability is very much a part of whom I am, but it doesn't make me who I am. So I'd be doing myself an injustice to constantly state the obvious every time I sit down and write. Everyone knows my situation by now, and it's like I said before, "If you don't believe me, check me out." What I'm saying is for all that don't know, won't know. After writing this book, I am not allowing myself to write about my disability anymore because in order to get this society to get over the whole myth about physical disabilities, I must first do it myself. How can I rightfully expect someone to buy what I'm selling if I don't buy it myself? I really do believe that it's a way for all of us to coexist.

But it's up to all of us to find what that way is. Then we all must be willing to do what we have to do to make it work. Nothing is ever accomplished when you try to do it alone. No man is an island. No matter how hard you try, you're always going to need help somewhere in your life. I'm not afraid to admit it, but what I want to do with regard to 3DO Stylez LLC and for the Will on Wheels, I need help. Help doesn't always refer to money, but it does take money to get things done. But more than that, it takes heart. If you have all the money and no heart, in my opinion, you have nothing. At least with heart, people will see the care and quality in everything you do. When that's all you have, you'll put your all into it. The best example I can give is college sports and professional sports. When you watch college kids play, they put their heart and soul in everything they do. because they know that if they want to, it takes 100 percent of everything you've got. But when they get to the pros, some get to the point to where they're going through the motions. But you can't do that; the same passion it takes to get there should be maintained in all you do. That's what I want to do every time I write or put an event together or work. I believe that a person, no matter who they are, should always be consistent and persistent if nothing else. A person who is unstable in everything they do can never be trusted, in my personal opinion. As I told you before, most of my learning experience didn't come from a classroom; it came from personal encounters with various kinds of people and situations. They're very few learning experiences that I can describe in detail, except for one. Most times, things happen in my life, and I move on having learned my lesson, never looking back on past successes or mistakes. The encounter that I had at five years old just eight months before my accident will stick with me for the rest of my life. People say everything happens for a reason. This is a very big reason why I look at life the way I do. My parents always taught me to think outside the box. That's the reason why they always exposed me to as much culture as they could, and my most memorable family vacation came at five years old. We took a road trip down to Florida for a three-week stay. While I was down there, I was given the opportunity to go in a real submarine and go sightseeing in the Atlantic Ocean. My dad and I was all for it. But my mom reluctantly said yes. So as we loaded into the submarine, I had no idea I was about to have a life-changing experience. As the sub immersed deeply into the water, my fear quickly changed into excitement. Before I knew it, I was in a whole another world. A whole another world where I thought air didn't exist to me. As I looked out the sub's window, I was able to see what's now today my most favorite animal in the world, sharks. Not only were their sharks, but also whales, dolphins, stingrays, and other species of fish and marine life that I'll never forget. Because of this experience, I believe anything in this world is possible to accomplish. I don't believe in I can't because I'm a living proof that if a guy like me can do it, anybody can. Especially if they have the full use of all their limbs, to me that's everything. To have the full use of your arms, legs, and hands and throw in a functioning brain, in my opinion, that's the recipe for ultimate weapons that possesses the ability to achieve anything if you want it bad enough. As you have been reading, there are many people and things in life that motivate me, but none have motivate more than a *gentleman* by the name of chef Jeff Henderson. This man has what I like to call a testimony and a half. He came from some very extreme situations that led to prison time. Now he's known as one of the greatest chef's in the world. Although I never met this man, just hearing his story makes me not want to give up on anything I do. Just because it seems like every door is slamming in my face and things may not be happening in my time, I must always remember that my time isn't God's time and delay isn't a denial. Earlier in my life, all I thought about was walking again, and my favorite thing to say used to be "what if," but it came a time in my life where I had to stop saying "what if" and start dealing with "what is." A while back, my mom asked me if do I ever think about walking again and do I still pray about it. The question kind of threw me off at first because after so long, not being able to walk became a natural part of my life. It's going to sound strange, but I guess after a while, I got comfortable with my situation.

The thought of walking became just a fantasy. I know that God can heal me at any time, but far as thinking about it and praying for my healing, I just don't think that it's that urgent for me to be able to walk. Of course, it'd be wonderful to be able to walk, but it's not a big deal to me. Some people would read this and say that I must be comfortable with being miserable, but that's not the case at all. I have a great life, better than most. As I get older, I've learned how to appreciate smaller things in life. Things like being able to hang out with my friend Jared, playing video games no matter how many times we beat it, it's just the fact we get to kick means the whole world to me. Being able to hang out with my family and reminisce on when time where much simpler. You know the things that we all take for granted when we're younger, but once we get older, we wish we had them back. Believe it or not, I've had my fair share of broken hearts involving the opposite sex. I told you I'm a know guy. Just 'cause I can't walk, you thought I never had a girl before? Oh yeah, just because I'm talking about this don't mean I'm naming names; LBJ ain't no fool either. If those females see their names in this book, they'd try to get money from me. That ain't happening! I'm a Barnett! Over the years, I've dealt with all types of pain. I have dealt with physical, emotional, and even some mental. But all of these things can't equal what I felt when I had a broken heart. Unfortunately, I've experienced four times;

I must say the last two times didn't hurt nearly as much as the first two. But it still hurt nonetheless. You know how they say that there is somebody for everybody. Well, I believe that's true, except for me. I'm not being negative about it, but given the track record, it just doesn't look like it's going to happen. There's too much extra stuff that comes along with being with someone in my situation. I'm finally at a place in my life where I can accept that. I'm not saying that it can't happen, I just don't believe it will.

I have no doubt that this woman exists, but sometimes I can't help but wonder, "Is she for me?" At the same time, there's something in me that won't let me give up hope totally. So I guess my best option, instead of looking so hard, is to let go and let God and continue to pray and wait. Even if it never happens, I must always understand that if it's not in God's plan, it's not meant to be. Besides that, you can't miss something you never had.

In that regard, I'm straight. Every missed opportunity that I've had in the past, I must look at them as God saving me from heartache that I didn't need. Let's just face it; my life hasn't exactly been a picnic, real talk.

I consider myself to be a realist. I don't believe in reading more into a situation than what's really there. It's like the old saying that goes "If it walks like a duck and quacks like a duck, it's a duck." This is the reason why I like to surround myself with real people. It's sad to say that nowadays it's not very many real people left. There's too many people walking around with a gimmick. This also pertains to people in relationships. People only care about what they can get and how fast they can get it. After they get what they want, they move on to the next victim. I've been victimized more times than I care to remember, and let me tell you, it hurts; but I also learned a lesson: Fool me once, shame on me. But what do you do when it happens a third, fourth, and fifth time? That's what you need to look out for. I had to get to a point in my life where I had to stop using my heart and start using my head. I don't know about you, but I don't want anyone else to make the mistake of thinking that they can take advantage of my situation or me. Don't let the wheelchair fool you. You're dealing with someone who's crippled, not stupid. You don't have any idea how many times I had to fight for everything I've accomplished. I've done too much to get what I have, and even though it may not look like much to you, I'm not about to give it up now. This is why it's so hard for me to trust people. I never know who's a vulture just waiting to pick me dry. I'm not being mean; I'm being cautious, don't get me wrong. I love meeting new people; I just don't like meeting fake people. When I meet you, come correct. Don't send your reps because nine times out of ten, I'll read right through that, and I'll try my best to expose you for the fraud you are. I believe in being one way with a person; if I like you, I like you. If I don't, I just don't. I do believe in being fair with everyone. I never judge a person based on what someone else said. If nothing else, everyone deserves at least one chance to prove him or herself. In my opinion, the best way to gain respect is to give it first. They're not many in my life I respect, but there's one in particular that I have a lot – for my cousin Sarah Saleem. Why her? You know how they say it ain't hard to find someone that actually gets you. Well, that person is Sarah. Sometimes it feels like people never understand what I'm saying, but when I tell it to my cousin, she gets it. I don't know why it is; it just is.

Some people you'll click with, and some you won't, no matter how hard you try, family or not. My cousin is the reason why I'm inspired to do a lot of stuff that I do. She's one of the people I really respect; I just wish we lived in the same state so we could communicate more often. I believe that it's a lot of stuff I could learn from her. That's something you won't hear me say about a lot of people. This may sound crazy, but a lot of the pain that I've felt in my life has been self-imposed. Why do I say that? Because I have done a lot of things in my life and I knew that they were not good for me. But I did it anyway because I just had to experience for myself and ended up hurting myself. So if I sound angry, it's because I'm more angry with myself for what I didn't do than I am at other people for what they did. This is another life's lesson that I had to learn in order to grow up. Because if you don't know, you can't grow. How can I rightfully help someone else if I can't help myself?

There is a very fine line between hunger and greed. Hunger makes you work harder to succeed. The more you stay hungry, the more you reduce the chances of becoming content. Because once you become content, you'll find yourself standing still while the whole world passes you by. I want to stop until I get there, but at the same time, I must keep myself balanced so that my hunger doesn't turn into greed. When a person is greedy, the greed will consume them until it ultimately destroys them. We must never make the mistake of thinking that success is meant just for us and no one else.

When we make that successful climb to the top of the mountain, always remember to throw the rope back so someone else can join you at the top. Never make the mistake of thinking that God's favor means you are God's favorite. Because we are all his children, his blessings are meant for all of us. I've got serious problem with anyone who gets arrogant just because they reached a certain status in life. Word for the wise: "Status positions and titles mean nothing if your mind and heart isn't right." Just to let you know, having your mind right doesn't mean cramming it full of useless information that you'll never use anyway. Having a right mind means changing your stinking thinking and knowing how to trust everyone right. No matter who they are and what they have, just remember, Jesus broke bread with sinners, and we all know that we're not above him. Even though some folks that I know think that they're on his level. News flash! You're not. I don't want anyone that reads this book to think that I'm antieducation or antigovernment, but there are a lot of things that go on in which I do not agree. All of my problems that I have with my own country stem from one question: Where do the physically disabled fit in in the good old USA. Do we even have a voice? If so, is anyone listening? Please don't get me any disrespect; it seems like no one cared until after Christopher Reeves couldn't walk. Now that he's gone, it feels like we're back at square one.

Sometimes square one isn't a bad place to be. Before I continue on, please allow me a moment to clear up my last statement when I say back at square one. I'm not saying that no progress has been made; what I mean is who's going to be our next spokesperson for people with physical disabilities.

Mr. Reeves had access to things that average people as myself can only dream of. Most people aren't going to understand what I'm about to say, but I'm a huge supporter of stem cell research. Reason being because I haven't walked in over twenty-two years. At this point in my life, if I'm given the chance to move again, even if it's nothing more than my arms and hands, I would be the happiest man in the world. Not being able to move anything make you feel like you're going crazy sometimes.

God has put in my life the perfect people, places, and things that keep me balanced, basically, to keep me from losing my mind. One of those places came at the very beginning of my journey: Denver Children's Hospital in Denver, Colorado. After everything I had been through in the prior months, they made me feel human again even though I was thousands of miles away from home. Folks in Denver went out of their way to make my parents and myself feel like family. But when I think about it, they did this for all of their patients. This place was so huge and so beautiful it felt more like a vacation resort than a hospital. How many hospitals you know with three full basketball courts, two Olympic-size pools, an arcade, and a movie-rental place, all under the same roof. I mean, sure it's probably the norm nowadays, but back in '86, it was cutting edge. This hospital is the place where I learned to think outside the box because of people like Dr. Mathews and two of my nurses, Teresa and Annie. These two nurses quickly became like family. It's because of them I learned how to communicate with people and hold conversations that actually made sense. They also taught me how to gamble, but that's a whole different story. I credit Denver, Colorado, for a lot of things that I do now. I hope and pray that those folks are doing well. Even if they all don't remember me, I know I'll never forget them. There comes a time in everyone's life when you have to show appreciation for the people who've positively influenced your life as a part of the growing and learning process. We all must realize that things people do for us are not done of obligation. Most times they're done out of love. Never make the mistake of thinking that people have to help us.

Sometimes they have the every right to say, "I'll forget you" and keep on moving along. If you don't understand that, then maybe you're not as smart as you think you are. You never know how you can brighten someone's day just by saying thank you or just by calling someone to see how he or she is doing. Keep in mind that sometimes it's the small things that count. I can't count how many times in my life I was sick in my room hoping the phone would ring and it would be someone on the other end calling to talk to me. I guess that's my problem. When I care about somebody, I probably care too much. Sometimes I wish I could say, "Forget it and keep moving ahead," but something inside of me won't allow me to do that. A special message to those people out there who has forgotten about me: "Thank you. It's because of your ignorance that makes me want to be great. Trust me, I won't stop until I finally get to where I want to be." One time in high school, we had a class discussion about who was average and who was above average. Someone had the audacity to say that I was average, and I didn't get angry, but I did look at the whole class and asked a point-blank question: "After knowing me for years, what part of my life says average?" At that point, the whole class got quiet. Because then they began to put themselves in my situation and began to realize not everyone can deal with what I go through every day. The more I think about it, the more I realize I don't want to be average. In my personal opinion, average is boring.

Life is one big roller coaster full of ups and downs, twists and turns, some situations that we face burn us so bad that we feel like giving up. Take it from me, no matter how tempting or easy it is, giving up is not the way. Because the moment you give up, you'll begin to wonder, "What if I gave up too soon?" As crazy as it may sound, it's easier to keep going forward than it is to start over. I'm the type of person that believes in making my situation work for me, instead of allowing the situation to work me. I talk a lot about education. Some good, some bad, but the bottom line is anyone reading this book must be able to come to their own conclusions. We've all got to get to the point in our lives when we stop allowing others to influence what we do. To all the young people out there, there's absolutely nothing wrong with being a trendsetter. Keep being who you are. Never lose your identity trying to impress somebody else. If people can't accept you for who you are, screw them. Please take a lesson from my life; if somebody crippled can do it, so can you. I have a lot of hopes and dreams; some may not. Nothing is guaranteed, but I will promise you this, I'm going to work my hardest to accomplish them all.

I suggest you do the same. Because if you don't, you'll be sitting around wondering what could've been. Even if you try and fail, at least you'll be able to say, "Hey, I tried. And had fun doing it!" Thank you for coming along with me on yet another journey.

Special thanks to all of the people who supported me while writing this book. Most of the names have been mentioned throughout the book. But for the ones who've not been mentioned, I'd rather keep that private. If anyone is asking the question, "Is there another book coming?" The answer's simple: I doubt it. It may be time for me to move on to something new, but you will be hearing a lot from me. I'm not that easy to get rid of.

LB Junior

Failure and rejection builds character; even though we may not want to accept it, we all have to face it. Nobody wants to fail, nobody wants to be rejected, but it comes with territory, I guess. I have been turned away and knocked down more times that I care to remember, but it is not how may times you get knocked down; it's how many times you get back up. Like what D-Wade said, "Get knocked down six times get up seven." Always remember that no one can be a better you than you; and no one can define you, but you. Please don't misunderstand what I am about to say, but most people really do suck – oh, it is harsh, but it is also true. What do I mean? Simply put, everybody is not in your corner, no matter what they say; just remember, smiling faces tell lies. When it comes to people that we let in our world, we must remember to keep the circle as small as possible, but at the same time keep friends close and keep enemies closer. Interesting concept because sometimes the enemy that we face is within ourselves. So here is the question: What are you going to do about it? Stand and fight or roll over and play dead.

This is who I am.
This is what makes me.
This is what I feel.

What I want so much should never hurt this bad. Maybe I'm on the right track after all.

FINAL THOUGHTS

WHEN I WAS faced down on the garage floor, I didn't know what the outcome would be. The only thing that I could say was Jesus helped me. Just like always, he came just in the nick of time. If you don't know anything else, always know Jesus, and please get to know him before it is too late. That situation that occurs on Saturday, May 10, 2008, could have turned out so different, but I thank God that I am still here. Life is beautiful.

The day after election day 2008, for the first time in my life, I feel like anything is possible. Simply put we have a black president, not of a major corporation, but of the USA. The only thing that I can say is Wow! This is living, breathing proof that you can do anything you set your mind to. November 4, 2008, will go down in history; it will forever be known as the day that the United States of America once again made history. There has always been a color line that people have been afraid to cross, but I can finally say the line has been broken. WOW, Will on the Wheels, now I can say let's go get it, 3 DO Stylez LLC. The future is now. April 25, 1986 was my stepping stone, not my stumbling block. Spitting through the wires with fire, I'm going higher. The sky is the limit, but if your mind isn't right, the limit is the sky. Yes, we can, and yes, we did. Thanks for the new motivation President Obama. The world is mine.

DORCHESTER*PUBLISHING*   200 Madison Avenue, Suite 2000 • NY, NY
10016

p 212.725.8811 f 212.532.1054

Dear Author,

Please be advised that Leisure Books is not currently acquiring original mystery/detective novels, erotica, science fiction, poetry, collections of short stories, anthologies. mainstream fiction, young adult fiction, women's fiction, or nonfiction.

Please excuse this printed form, but due to the sheer volume of submissions we cannot send a personal reply.

Best of luck finding another publisher.

Sincerely,

Alissa Davis

Alissa D. Davis
Editorial Assistant

 # PELICAN PUBLISHING COMPANY

1000 BURMASTER STREET GRETNA, LA 70053

October 15, 2008

Dear Author:

Thank you for your recent submission to Pelican Publishing Company. We regret to inform you that the material does not meet our needs at this time.

Since your submission did not include the customary self-addressed stamped envelope for the return of materials, it is unclear whether you expect your submission to be returned or recycled. If you want it to be returned, we will need a SASE large enough to accommodate it or a check for the appropriate amount of postage.

We will hold your material for four weeks after the date of this letter. If we don't hear from you in that time, we will assume that you do not need the material back and it will be recycled.

We appreciate your interest in Pelican Publishing and wish you the best as you pursue publication.

Sincerely,
The Editors

Triple Crown Publications

2184 Citygate Drive
Columbus, OH 43219

614.478.9402
614.478.9458 fax

October 13, 2008

Mr. Larry Barnett, Jr.
1409 Lamont St.
Saginaw, MI 48601

Dear Larry,

This letter acknowledges, with thanks, your recent submissions to Triple Crown Publications. Unfortunately, your manuscript does not fit the genre of books in our collection.

We publish urban Hip Hop fiction, and although we appreciate the time and effort many writers of other versions of urban literature or genres (such as autobiographies or poetry) invest to send us their manuscripts, we regret to inform them that we cannot see these manuscripts standing within our catalog.

Again, we thank you for taking the time to send us your manuscript, and we wish you the best in your future writing endeavors.

Sincerely,
Submissions Department
Triple Crown Publications

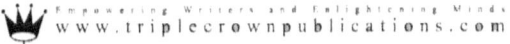

Empowering Writers and Enlightening Minds
www.triplecrownpublications.com

HarperOne
A Division of
HarperCollins*Publishers*

| 353 Sacramento Street
| Suite 500
| San Francisco, California
| 94111-3653

Telephone 415 477-4400
Fax 415 477-4444
E-mail harperone@harpercollins.com
Web Site www.harperone.com

September 30, 2008

Larry Barnett Jr.
1409 Lamont St.
Saginaw, MI 48601

Dear Larry,

Thank you for sending the proposal for *Welcome to My Life* for consideration for future publication. Unfortunately, we do not see it fitting on our upcoming lists. We must be incredibly careful to choose those projects that best match our marketing and publishing strengths.

Thank you for thinking of HarperOne, and we wish you the best of luck in finding a worthy publisher.

Sincerely,

Michael G. Maudlin
V.P. & Editorial Director
HarperOne, an imprint of HarperCollins Publishers

S I M O N & S C H U S T E R

1230 Avenue of the Americas
New York, NY 10020
212-698-7000

Dear Author:

We have received your recent inquiry concerning submission of a manuscript to Simon & Schuster. Due to the volume of submissions it is not possible for our editorial staff to read manuscripts that have not been submitted by a literary agent.

We regret that we cannot recommend specific agents for your work, but a directory of literary agents is one section of *Literary Market Place*, a reference work published by RR Bowker that can be found in most libraries. In your search for a literary agent you should look for someone who will make an effort to place your work with a publishing house most compatible with the content and style of your work.

We wish you success in finding a home for your manuscript and than you for thinking of Simon & Schuster.

Sincerely,

Editorial Department
Simon & Schuster Adult Publishing Group

ALPHA BOOKS

800 East 96th Street, 3rd Floor
Indianapolis, IN 46240

November 5, 2008

Larry Bennett, Jr.
1409 Lamont Street
Saginaw, MI 48601

Dear Larry,

Thank you for the opportunity to review your proposal; *Welcome to My Life.*

Unfortunately, we do not publish biographical titles.

I wish you luck with another publisher.

Sincerely,

Jill Thomas,
Sr. Editorial Coordinator
Alpha Books

/jdt

February 16, 2005

To whom it may concern:

My name is Larry Barnett Jr. I'm the president of 3 DO Records. I am interested in renting two facilities of the Saginaw Public Schools: Saginaw High School Auditorium or Arthur Hill High School auditorium.

The purpose of the rental is to host the "2nd Annual Christian Youth Explosion." Rudy E. Barnett, president of Vessel Entertainment, and myself will compromise this event. The title of this youth explosion is "Celebration of Life."

We're expected to seat around 200 to 250 guests. If possible, the date to host this event will be Sunday, June 4, 2005. The facility will be in use from 3:00 p.m. to 10:00 p.m. with the event beginning at 5:00 p.m. to 9:00 p.m.

The equipment to be used, such as keyboards, amplifiers, and microphones will be supplied by Vessel Entertainment. The only assistance needed from the school will be lighting.

Denied

MY HEART

TWO OF THE most painful parts of life are failure and rejection. I have dealt with both. I truly believe that my life's worth is my willingness to work harder than anyone else I know. Although these are not my words, they speak volumes to my situation. Too many people take for granted the small things in life without realizing how blessed they really are. Please live your life to the absolute fullest and never look back.

I am going to ride this thing called life until the wheels fall off, believe that pimpin'.

Who says that success is not for me. Anybody that makes this statement is clearly my enemy. The title of this book is *Schools In*. Why? Because people need to learn that no matter the obstacle, you can overcome anything. The other reason for this book is to give those folks, who think that they are better because of what they think, a reality check and tell them that they are full of crap.

No matter how far you go in life, the learning process is never over. There will always be some lessons to learn in life and just when you think you have it all figured out, here comes another situation to pull you back down to earth.

In the words of my favorite rapper, Nas, "You gotta stay true to who you are and where you come from or at the top will be the same place you hang from."

Simply put, keep it real in everything you do. Always stay humble and always keep God first. No position in life is bigger than God. Please remember that he is the reason why you have what you have.

GO HARD or GO HOME, says Saginaw's FINEST.

Impacted by

1. Malcolm X
2. Mr. Willie Thompson
3. Rev. Dr. Martin Luther King Jr.
4. President Barrack Obama
5. Langston Hughes

Inspired By

1. The Jordan Rules
2. Michael Jordan, the 2nd Coming
3. Kanye West, *Graduation*
4. T.I., *Paper Trail*
5. Akon, *Freedom*
6. Nas, *God's Son*
7. Dr. Cornell West

TRUTHFUL

I have little or
no use for fake
people; the only
people that I
want to be
connected to are
the real ones.
This is what I
call real talk, I
pride myself on
This way of life.
Always stay true
to everyone.

EVERY MAN, WOMAN, and
child has a dream. What that

dream is, I don't know; that is between you and God. The only thing I can say is that you should go for it no matter what people have to say. People can't judge you, only God can. The more people talk, the more I want to prove them wrong.

The bottom line is this: people who judge others suck. They are unhappy, and they want everyone else to be unhappy. These miserable folks have a lot of free-floating anger and they always blame others for their own failures. Well, in the words of Master P, it ain't my fault. If you fail don't blame others. In fact, don't blame anybody. Just pick yourself and start over. Circumstances do not dictate your future. If a person chooses to have a pity party, let them know that it will be a party for one if they choose to have that   same party every day. It took me a long time to understand that life is meant to be enjoyed, and every time I talked about the past, I ran folks away. Word for the wise: Please let the old crap go.

Every man, woman, and child has a dream. What that dream is, I don't know; that is between you and God. The only thing I can say is that you should go for it no matter what people have to say. People can't judge you, only God can. The more people talk, the more I want to prove them wrong.

The bottom line is this: people who judge others suck. They are unhappy, and they want everyone else to be unhappy. These miserable folks have a lot of free-floating anger and they always blame others for their own failures. Well, in the words of Master P, it ain't my fault. If you fail don't blame others. In fact, don't blame anybody. Just pick yourself and start over. Circumstances do not dictate your future. If a person chooses to have a pity party, let them know that it will be a party for one if they choose to have that   same party every day. It took me a long time to understand that life is meant to be enjoyed, and every time I talked about the past, I ran folks away. Word for the wise: Please let the old crap go.

I pretty much suck at everything I set out to do: WOW 3 DO Records LLC, college, relationships, I mean everything. If it sounds like I'm being negative, I'm not. What I'm doing is giving myself a wake-up call because sometimes that is what it takes to make yourself see things for what they really are.

I guess you can call it a self reality check. Besides that, how many people you know that are real enough to stand up and straighten themselves out. This will be the realist stuff I ever wrote. Even though I'm a failure, I will never be a loser because even when winning sounds illogical, losing is still far from optional. As long as I try my best and work my *hardiest*, I will never ever lose. Please don't give up on your dreams too easy and realize the real potential that God has put in you. Then you have those people in life that think that they are better than everybody else; these people are the real losers. My folks always taught me that everybody is equal in the eyes of God, no matter if you have 6 billion dollars or if you have 6 cents to your name. God does not care about social status or any of the other materialistic garbage that we think is so important.

I mean, look at it this way Jesus talked to, ate with, walked with, and healed sinners, so who do we think we are to put ourselves above anybody? If you ask me the people that claim to do the right thing are the ones doing wrong because these people are the ones judging others without knowing the whole story, correct me if I am wrong but I always thought that only God can judge me, get this God is the leader not Gordon, Gayle, or anybody else's name that just happens to start with the letter *G*. People have the "I am everything" complex, but just remember that the devil has the same problems and just look at where he is headed. Just because you may have a little more than somebody else does not make you better. Don't get it twisted. God's favor does not make you his favorite; he has no favorites because we are all winners no matter what we do. Now that's what school is all about. See you next book.

NEVER UNDER ESTIMATE ANYONE THEY JUST MIGHT PROVE YOU WRONG.

www.ingramcontent.com/pod-product-compliance
Lightning Source LLC
Chambersburg PA
CBHW031301280526
45784CB00004B/1935